For all the little adventurers who know that love is the biggest adventure of all!

Every creature, big or small, has a special way to say: 'I love you.' Let's discover their stories together!

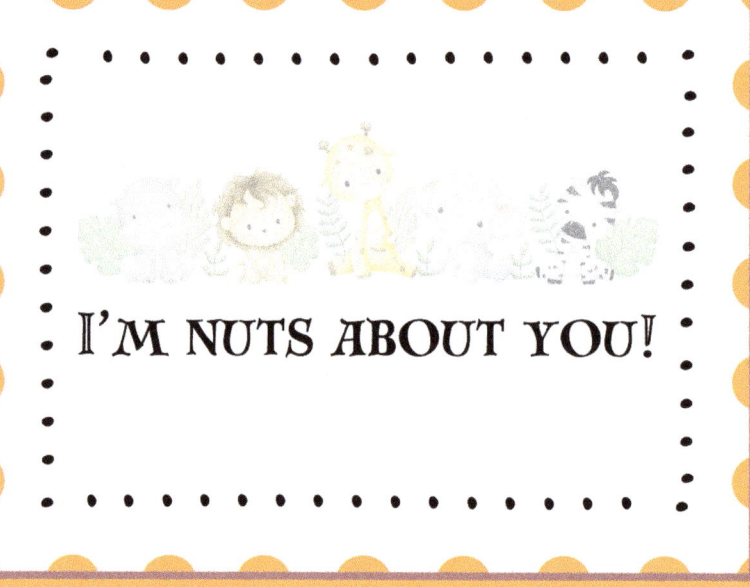

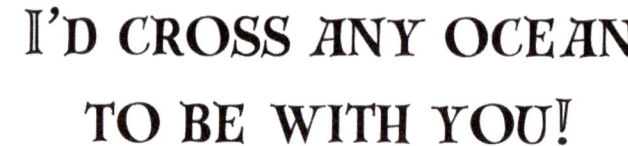

I'D CROSS ANY OCEAN
TO BE WITH YOU!

I'M NEVER IN A RUSH TO SHOW YOU MY LOVE.

Our bond is un-frog-ettable!

You're my favorite cuddle-bunny!

You're the coolest penguin in my world!

You're totally clawsome!

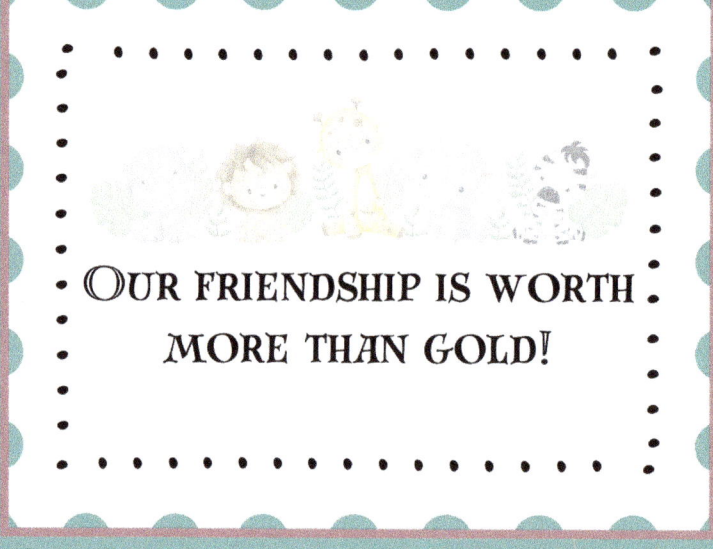

OUR FRIENDSHIP IS WORTH MORE THAN GOLD!

We're better together,
just like a flock.

I'LL ALWAYS STICK WITH YOU, NO MATTER WHAT.

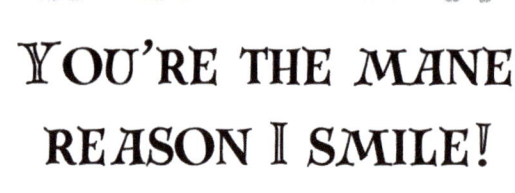

You're the mane reason I smile!

Sharing brings us closer, like the river brings life to all.

Bee-cause of you, my heart feels light.

Paws together, we're the perfect team!

HOPPING THROUGH FIELDS OF COLOR, SIDE BY SIDE FOREVER.

You're my purr-fect friend, through and through.

Together, we soar, just me and you.

Thank You! ♥

We are so grateful that you chose our book to bring joy and creativity into your life! Your support means the world to us, and we're thrilled to have been a part of your storytime and imagination.

Every page you've explored celebrates the beauty of friendship, kindness, and love. We hope our illustrations and words brought smiles, giggles, and magical moments to you and your little ones.
Your choice to share this journey with us fills our hearts with happiness. It's not just a book—it's a connection, and we're honored to be a part of your creative world.

Thank you for being part of this wonderful adventure. Keep spreading love and kindness wherever you go!

www.ingramcontent.com/pod-product-compliance
Lightning Source LLC
Chambersburg PA
CBHW061120170426
43209CB00013B/1617